Four Witnesses, One Gospel?

Reflections on the Fourfold Gospel and the Revised Common Lectionary

Andrew F Gregory

Research Fellow in New Testament, Keble College, Oxford

GROVE BOOKS LIMITED
RIDLEY HALL RD CAMBRIDGE CB3 9HU

Contents

1. Reading the Bible in Church 3
2. Four Gospels as a Theological and Historical Challenge 6
3. Weave Them All Together: Harmonization 11
4. The Complex Unity of the Fourfold Gospel 16
5. Gospel Unity and the Revised Common Lectionary 18
6. The Portrait Analogy 20
7. Preaching the Gospel from the Gospels *by Philip Jenson* 23
   Notes 25

Acknowledgements

I am grateful to Robert Morgan and to members of the Grove Biblical Group, especially Keith Grüneberg and Philip Jenson, for their comments on an earlier draft of this text. They made many suggestions for its improvement, but the responsibility for any remaining obscurities or other infelicities remains, of course, my own. Particular thanks go to Philip Jenson, who contributed chapter seven.

A Note on Terminology

The word 'gospel' is used both of God's good news about the life, death and resurrection of Jesus (usually—and originally—a message proclaimed by word of mouth) and also of written accounts of the ministry and significance of Jesus in which that message was recorded. In what follows I use Gospel (upper-case G) for this message, but gospel (lower-case g) for written narrative accounts of the ministry and significance of Jesus.

The Cover Illustration is by Peter Ashton

Copyright © Andrew Gregory and Philip Jenson 2005

First Impression June 2005
ISSN 1365-490X
ISBN 1 85174 595 5

Reading the Bible in Church 1

The size of the Bible and the wide range of material that it contains means that it is not practical—and perhaps not even desirable—to read it in its entirety in the course of Sunday worship, even over a large number of years.

Therefore different churches adopt different approaches to try to achieve a principled and coherent approach to the reading of the Bible in public worship. One approach is to use a lectionary, a carefully chosen list of readings appointed for use on specific occasions in the church year. Not only does this offer the advantage of a well-balanced diet of Scripture, it also means that Christians in any one congregation that uses the lectionary are reading the same Scriptures at the same time as many other Christians, a helpful reminder of their place in a church that extends across the world.

It is a helpful reminder to Christians in any one congregation of their place in a church that extends across the world

The lectionary most widely used in the English-speaking western church is the *Revised Common Lectionary*. Its purpose is clear and well known—it aims to acquaint congregations with as much of Scripture as practically possible. In order to do so, it offers a three-year cycle of Sunday readings in which each year is centred on a semi-continuous reading of one synoptic gospel (that is, in each year we read most, but not all, of one of Matthew, Mark or Luke, usually in the order that each passage occurs in the gospel in which it is found).[1] Exceptions to this pattern include certain key points where, depending on one's assessment, each synoptic account is supplemented, interrupted or illuminated by John. We may ask whether the lectionary should follow a cycle of four years rather than of three,[2] yet setting John alongside each of the synoptic gospels illustrates the theological conviction that John may be read in such a way that it complements rather than conflicts with the synoptic gospels. This recurrent juxtaposition of John and one of the synoptic gospels offers a potentially fruitful dynamic that might easily be lost were John allocated—or relegated to?—a year of its own.[3]

The RCL is used by a wide range of churches, sometimes with local variations. This is the case in the Church of England, where the new pattern marks a distinctive change from the lectionary contained in the *Alternative Service Book* (ASB; a prayer book used in the Church of England as an alternative to the *Book of Common Prayer* in the period 1980 to 2000). The ASB lectionary was based on a two-year cycle that moved between gospels, juxtaposing texts from all four canonical gospels and elsewhere to illustrate certain themes. The way in which the new lectionary works is different, however. It sets out to present the distinctive emphases and particular insights of each evangelist (*ie* gospel writer) in the context of the liturgical reading of Scripture.[4] Rather than attempt in any one year to focus primarily on a composite picture of Jesus, it offers an opportunity to foreground instead the theological perspective of each evangelist and the distinctive witness to Jesus that he bears, but in a framework that includes material from other gospels as well.

Benefits...and Distractions?

From an educational perspective, there are many benefits from such an approach. First, it increases the amount of Scripture that is read. Second, it brings the lectionary of the church into line with those trends in New Testament scholarship that illuminate the distinctive interests of each evangelist. Third, it goes some way towards providing a liturgical framework for an increased appreciation of each gospel as a literary whole. Yet, important as such academic insights may be, both in the church and in the academy, it is not clear that they should be the most important influences on the liturgical reading of Scripture and the preaching of the church. Certainly preachers will benefit from a critical and detailed engagement with such scholarship, and it is to be hoped that preachers give appropriate consideration to such insights. Such work will help to shape and inform not only sermons but also those who hear them, even (perhaps especially) if preachers make no explicit reference to the commentaries and other academic work on which they have drawn.

> *Education aimed at biblical literacy is not necessarily suited primarily or exclusively to the pulpit and lectionary*

Nevertheless education aimed at biblical literacy is not necessarily suited primarily or exclusively to the pulpit and lectionary. There may be dangers if concerns for such literacy lead preachers and worshipping congregations to focus on the distinctive emphases and concerns of the evangelists to the extent that they lose sight of the Jesus to whom the evangelists bear witness. Biblical literacy, and therefore an appreciation of the gospels, is certainly to be encouraged. But the question is how best it may be done, and whether it is reasonable to expect that it all takes place in the context of the liturgy. The education of Christians is important, for adults as well as for children. But such education is only one part of what Christians refer to as discipleship, a pattern of learning that has at its centre a lifelong relationship with Jesus. So if Christian preaching is to focus on Christ crucified, then the question arises of how in our worship we make most responsible use of our primary written sources about Jesus in order to focus not on the sources but on the one to whom those sources bear witness.

Such education is only one part of a pattern of learning that has at its centre a lifelong relationship with Jesus

Questions

- How much is the lectionary used in your church? Is another means of choosing Bible readings used instead? Which approach do you prefer, and why?
- What kind of plan do you use for reading the Bible yourself? Is it a balanced one?

2 Four Gospels as a Theological and Historical Challenge

For those of us who are already accustomed to working with four gospels, it may be difficult to appreciate the extent of the difficulties caused by the fact that more than one gospel was written and accepted as authoritative.

As Oscar Cullmann puts it, 'The fact that the church takes the fourfold canon of the gospels for granted makes it difficult for us to see how the matter ever became a problem at all.'[5] Yet, as Graham Stanton observes, 'the decision to accept four gospels, along with the earlier acceptance of a plurality of gospels, was one of the most momentous ones taken within early Christianity, a decision which cries out for continuing theological reflection.'[6]

Undergirding the church's memory and proclamation of Jesus Christ—the Gospel, to adopt the pre-Pauline terminology that Christians still use today[7]—is a fundamental theological conviction that there is one Jesus presented to us in four different written gospels that have been recognized as Scripture and included in the New Testament. The canon of four written gospels and the uniform titles that they carry testify to the belief that there is but one Gospel of Jesus Christ, although presented in four forms: the (one) Gospel according to Matthew, to Mark, to Luke and to John. Other gospels may be important for other reasons, especially to historians of early Christianity. However, they carry no theological authority for the worshipping community that bases its understanding of itself and of the world on 'the Gospel of Jesus Christ as witnessed to by Paul, by Mark and by other early Christians later deemed to belong to the circle of apostles and their followers.'[8] For, as Stanton observes, a gospel is not Gospel 'when it is a set of Jesus traditions out of kilter with the faith of the church.'[9]

The privileged place that the church affords to the four gospels and the one fourfold Gospel is often challenged today

Yet the fourfold Gospel was not always taken for granted, even within the church. Furthermore, the privileged place that the church affords to the four gospels and the one fourfold Gospel is often challenged today. Therefore it may be helpful to step back to consider other options that the church might have made had not it chosen to adopt the fourfold Gospel as its authoritative narrative account of the ministry and significance of Jesus. A consideration of these other options should help us see what is distinctive about the fourfold Gospel.

At least four possible responses might be made to the fact that so many gospels and related texts have been written about Jesus. Each can be seen to have emerged as early as the second century. The first is that we are open to any gospel, subject to careful consideration of its merits. The second is the opposite approach, choosing one gospel and one gospel alone. The other options offer different ways of holding more than one gospel together: conflating them into one larger harmonized narrative; or holding them together in some form of creative tension. In what remains of this chapter I shall consider the first and second of these responses; the third and fourth are the subject of chapters three and four.

Take Each Gospel On Its Merits: Critical Openness

To describe the most inclusive approach to assessing the potential value of the many gospels that have been written as one of 'anything goes' would be unfair. Much more helpful is to speak of taking each gospel on its own merits. Inevitably, such judgments will depend on the use to which a reader wants to put a gospel, and the criteria that each reader employs in judging the text. For an example of such critical openness in the second-century we might turn to Serapion, Bishop of Antioch.[10]

Although probably writing at a time after Irenaeus had already defended the fourfold Gospel,[11] Serapion was prepared—at least initially—to countenance the use of a certain *Gospel of Peter* in a church in his diocese, despite the fact that he was unfamiliar with its contents. Serapion seems to have thought that its name and the title to apostolic authority that it claimed was sufficient reason to suppose that it might have some use in the life of the church. Only later, after an examination of the text, does Serapion take a more cautious line. Even then, however, his refutation of the false teaching contained in this text is presented alongside the evaluation that most of it is quite acceptable.

What seems much more important is that Serapion has a clear conception of what the Gospel actually is

Serapion does appear to have other authoritative texts that allow him to decide which parts of the *Gospel of Peter* are acceptable and which are not, but the fact that he has some form of authority to refer to—perhaps even the fourfold Gospel—does not yet mean that other texts are excluded simply because they are not the gospels associated with

Matthew, Mark, Luke or John.[12] If Serapion has a gospel canon, it is not an exclusive one. What seems much more important is that he has a clear conception of what the Gospel actually is. Thus it is this prior commitment to a particular understanding of the story and significance of Jesus that allows him to assess whether other written gospels conform to the Gospel proclaimed by and handed down in the church. Just as Paul could refer to the one Gospel of Jesus Christ long before the four (and other) gospels were written, so the rule of faith[13]—the Gospel—that is preserved in those gospels determines the criteria by which other gospels should be evaluated.

When we turn to the contemporary situation, we find that there are many scholars who are also open to the use of non-canonical gospels, both for historical and theological purposes.[14] One of the most controversial topics in the study of these texts is the question of whether they are earlier or later than the canonical gospels. Two recent treatments of the historical Jesus show the very different ways in which such sources may be assessed.

Assessing the Sources
John P Meier offers an extensive and detailed discussion of these texts in his account of potential sources in the quest of the historical Jesus.[15] He addresses them on what he considers to be their merits, but concludes that non-canonical sources are late and tell us little about the historical Jesus. They draw on the canonical gospels, but not on any significant historical information that is independent of them.

Dominic Crossan offers a different account of the historical Jesus, including in his work an appendix in which he puts the sources in strata according to how close they are to the historical Jesus.[16] Stratum 1, the earliest evidence, which Crossan dates 30–60, contains the letters of Paul, and a number of non-canonical gospels and postulated sources of the canonical gospels. Stratum 2, dated 60–80 contains other non-canonical gospels, as well as Mark. Matthew and Luke are in stratum 3, dated 80–120, and followed also by John.

These different approaches raise acutely questions about how we are to date our sources for Jesus

These different approaches raise acutely questions about how we are to date our sources for Jesus. Crossan is a leading proponent of one recent development in scholarship, particularly in North America, which seeks to give such texts a more important place than their canonical counterparts in the attempt to learn more about the historical Jesus. He addresses these texts on what he considers to be their merits, arguing that they are earlier than and independent of the canonical gospels. Hence he finds in them much that allows him to penetrate behind what he considers to be the distorted figure of Jesus who is portrayed in traditional Christian piety, and thus to see Jesus as he really was.

Yet Crossan does not enter into debate with those who take different views on whether these sources are earlier than and independent of the canonical gospels so his position 'is presumed, not proved.'[17] Crossan is typical of a perception in certain predominantly North American circles that—if I may paraphrase George Orwell—canonical texts are bad, but non-canonical texts are good. Yet, as Meier and others have demonstrated, there is little reason on historical grounds to argue that such texts will cast much, if any, fresh light on either the historical Jesus or the earliest traditions that arose as a result of his impact on the earliest generations of his followers. Meier and Crossan both set out to approach these texts as historians, judging them on their merits, but reach very different conclusions when they do so—and there is little doubt Meier has the surer methodological foundation on which to base his historical conclusions.

Choose Just One Gospel: Radical Reductionism

If an attitude of potential openness to a whole range of texts is at one end of the spectrum, then its opposite is the decision to use one gospel text and one gospel alone. Irenaeus claims that a number of groups whom he considers heretical were distinguished by their exclusive or predominant use of one gospel text rather than of four.[18] Questions may be raised as to whether this claim owes more to Irenaeus' rhetoric than to the defining characteristic of such groups. But there is no reason to doubt that Marcion used only what appears to have been a short version of Luke, and that he identified this text as containing the one Gospel preached by Paul. As Oscar Cullmann observes, Marcion 'gave classical expression to the principle that there could only be one Gospel. As chief witness he quotes the apostle Paul, who speaks of the Gospel in the singular in Romans 2.16, thereby clearly indicating that anything apart from the one Gospel must be a forgery.'[19]

This is striking testimony to the impact of the fourfold Gospel

There are many people today whom we might loosely call Marcionite because in practice they reject the Jewish Scriptures (as Marcion also did), even if in theory they accept them. But it is difficult to find a contemporary example of someone who, like Marcion, would champion the exclusive use of only one gospel. This is striking testimony to the impact of the fourfold Gospel. Many of us may picture Jesus in a manner that is more like the portrayal of one evangelist than of another—and perhaps we might prefer Luke as Marcion did, though perhaps for very different reasons. Yet few of us are likely to defend such an approach in the way that Marcion appears to have done. There may be particular contemporary situations in which only gospel is used at a specific time—the distribution of a single gospel in the context of evangelism, or the use of a single gospel in the context of catechesis—but in such cases no-one is implying that a single gospel used in this way is the only gospel whose witness ought to be allowed.

If Serapion and Marcion represent two apparent extremes in their approach to the multiplicity of gospel texts that were available in the second century, two other responses each offer a different approach. One is harmonization; the other is the adoption of the fourfold Gospel. Each shares with the Marcionite approach an attempt to reduce the number of authoritative sources from the many sources that were available, but each does so by attempting in different ways to hold together the four gospels now considered canonical. These are the subjects of chapters three and four.

> ## Questions
> - Which is your preferred gospel—and why?
> - Imagine a New Testament with only one of our four gospels in it. What would be lost if the other three were absent? How would you feel about this? You might want to answer these questions for each gospel in turn.

Weave Them All Together: Harmonization   3

Harmonization tackles the problems posed by the existence of more than one gospel by weaving them together into one sequential narrative.

By far the most important example is that of Tatian, whose gospel harmony, known as the *Diatessaron* has been hugely influential. No copies of the original text survive, so our knowledge of its content depends on a range of later witnesses. However, there seems no reason to doubt that Tatian managed to use most of the substance of the canonical gospels and to weave together their content in a framework dominated by Matthew and by John. Here already we see the kind of conflation familiar still from Christmas carol services or services on Good Friday that use Jesus' seven last words from the cross. Yet unlike the 'mini-harmonies' used in such services, Tatian harmonized the gospels comprehensively and systematically.

Tatian harmonized the gospels comprehensively and systematically

This approach of moving between gospels and drawing them into one continuous whole without regard for their individual distinctiveness and particular content and structure is perhaps not too far removed from many unreflective approaches to the gospels today. Thus it is an integral component of many contemporary expressions of personal piety or spirituality, and the foundation on which many perceptions of Jesus' ministry are built. Such unreflective harmonization has its drawbacks, but it should not be rejected out of hand in either its popular or more critical forms. Those who move unselfconsciously from one portrayal of Jesus to another may not offer any explicit theological rationale for doing so, but what they do often reflects and implies both the theological conviction of the unity of Scripture, and the historical conviction that these four sources bear witness to one individual. The strength of this approach may be the way in which it is used to build up a picture of the one Jesus behind the four gospels considered authoritative for the life of the community of faith. But its weakness

The strength of this approach may be the way in which it is used to build up a picture of the one Jesus behind the four gospels

is the way in which it diminishes the distinctiveness of the different literary portrayals through which Jesus may be encountered today.

For the purpose of this discussion, at least three possible reactions to the differences between the gospels may be noted. Two are clearly types of harmonization, and I shall refer to them as 'circumstantial' and 'chronological.' Closely related to them is a third response to the differences between the gospels that I shall characterize as 'theological.' This theological approach takes note of distinctive emphases within each gospel and of apparent discrepancies between them, and attempts to account for them by holding them together in a way that does not collapse the accounts into one undifferentiated and univocal narrative such as that of Tatian. Thus it refuses to move too quickly to present a portrait of a composite Jesus that glosses over the differences between the gospels, and the opportunities for, and challenges to, theological reflection and preaching that such differences present.

Circumstantial Harmonization

By circumstantial harmonization, I mean small details in the narrative that may be harmonized without changing substantially the significance of different accounts in different gospels. For example, there is little at stake if we refer to the rich young ruler thus conflating Luke's account of a rich ruler, (Lk 18.18–24) with that of Matthew's account of a rich young man (Mt 19.16–22) who asks Jesus what he should do to inherit life. The point of the encounter remains the same, and there is little or nothing (christological or otherwise) at stake in the evangelists' different descriptions of Jesus' interlocutor.

Chronological Harmonization

Much more significant is harmonization of a chronological nature, by which I mean the attempt to take the gospels apart and then to put them back together as one continuous account of as much of the life and ministry of Jesus as may be accessible. Such harmonization treats the gospels not as distinct and discrete portrayals, but as pieces of a larger jigsaw puzzle which should be assembled in order to produce one comprehensive life of Jesus on the basis of four or more accounts.

Such harmonization is usually driven by a particular understanding of the importance of historical trustworthiness and the way in which such trustworthiness demands a particular correspondence between texts and the people and events that they portray. But though often attempted, it may undermine

Though often attempted, it may undermine much of what the different evangelists set out to achieve

much of what the different evangelists set out to achieve. To harmonize in one chronological account Jesus' words from the cross not only obscures the way in which each evangelist uses Jesus' last words to bring to an appropriate climax the life and ministry that their narrative of Jesus portrays, but also implies a claim about the nature of these texts and their relationship to events outside the text that none of the evangelists set out to make.[20]

Our familiarity with such systematic if limited harmonizations may blind us to the difficulties that they create, but any attempt to create a systematic harmony of the four gospels that is biographical and chronological in nature and comprehensive in scope quickly reaches very substantial difficulties. This can be seen both in respect of the synoptic gospels, and also of their relationship to John.[21] Questions that arise as a result of the comparison of the synoptic accounts concern the manner in which the individual evangelists present the same or similar sayings and events in different ways. There may be good reason to suppose that Jesus spoke the Beatitudes and the Lord's Prayer in different forms on different occasions, but what did Jesus say and do at the Last Supper, and in what order (with Mk 14.22–25 and Mt 26.26–29 compare Lk 22.14–22, noting textual variants, and 1 Cor 11.23–26)? Questions that concern the relationship between John and the synoptics include the timing of Jesus' cleansing of the temple (was it at the first of more than one Passover that Jesus observed in Jerusalem, so Jn 2.13–16, or was it immediately prior to the Passover before which he was crucified, as in Mk 11.15–18, Mt 21.12–16, Lk 19.45–48)? Or on what date did Jesus die (after the Passover meal, as in the synoptics, or before the meal, when the Passover lambs were slain, as in John)?

Theological Harmonization

Such questions are not unimportant, but they lead to insurmountable problems only when we treat the gospels as sources for a biographical narrative of the life of Jesus that follows the conventions of *modern* history writing. They are much less problematic when we read the gospels as *ancient* biographies or as testaments to the impact that Jesus made on those who followed him.[22] If we read them in this way, we can treat the canonical gospels as complementary but essentially harmonious portraits of one life, not as jigsaw pieces that can be pulled part and then reconstructed into one closed, continuous and harmonized whole.

Thus the third response to the plurality of the canonical gospels and the nature of their differing witness to Jesus might be described as literary (taking seriously the gospels as narrative texts, each to be read in its own right) and as theological (taking seriously the central convictions that they convey). This approach notes different emphases and perspectives between each of the gospels.

But, rather than seeking to fit them together into one continuously ordered narrative, it asks instead how we may account for these differences. It takes seriously not only the conviction that all four accounts witness to the impact of one person, but also that this impact has been presented in different ways by each of the evangelists. It recognizes that their desire to communicate the significance of Jesus to the different audiences for whom they probably wrote is likely to have affected the way in which the evangelists understood and presented their accounts. Therefore it takes seriously any knowledge that we have about the reasons that they wrote: to proclaim the significance of Jesus, not just—if in fact at all—to give an outline of his life. John and Luke each make this clear in direct and explicit address to their hearers (John 20.30–31; Luke 1.3–4) and a similar general purpose may reasonably be attributed also to Matthew and to Mark. Therefore apparent chronological discrepancies between gospels such as the day on which Jesus died may easily be accounted for if we read them as different ways of making the same point, that Jesus' death is to be associated with God's saving action as exemplified in the Passover and its celebration.

A theologically sensitive reading of the texts is a reading that approaches the gospels for what they are

Thus a theologically sensitive reading of the texts (which is a reading that is also sensitive to the historical and literary form of those texts) is a reading that approaches the gospels for what they are. Such a reading focuses not on discrepancies between the gospels but on the point that each evangelist appears to wish to make in the context of his gospel as a whole. As a consequence, there is no need to create a harmonious chronological reconstruction of the events behind the texts. Instead we recognize that we have no access to those events save in so far as they are recorded for us by the sources at our disposal (primarily the canonical evangelists, but also Paul). So we realize that if we create a harmony extracted from those witnesses, then we create an additional layer of tradition that distances us further from the Jesus to whom these sources bear witness, not a means by which we can get behind our literary sources and therefore closer to the Jesus whom they portray.

This is the reason that the church gave a privileged place in the canon to the fourfold Gospel rather than to Tatian's *Diatessaron*, and why the fourfold Gospel is to be preferred to any attempt to weave the gospels together. Continuing use of the fourfold Gospel means that we neither add to nor take away from the canonical gospels that the church accepts as authoritative. It also provides a framework in which we may acknowledge and explore both the points on which the gospels differ and those on which they agree.

The origins of this response to the problem of the existence of four similar but different accounts of the significance of Jesus' life, death and resurrection are the subject of chapter four.

> ## Question
> If you were asked to give a brief account of the story of Jesus, which incidents from his ministry would you select? Would one gospel be primary? If so, what incidents would be from other gospels?

4 The Complex Unity of the Fourfold Gospel

Hold Authoritative Accounts Together

The fourth approach, the use of a fourfold Gospel, has its first clearly datable advocate in Irenaeus, who was Bishop of Lyons in the late second century. Contemporary, or perhaps slightly later, are the first surviving examples of the use of the uniform style of title for these texts, 'the Gospel according to Matthew,' '…Mark' and so on. This formulation is found both in early gospel codices and (at least in an approximate form) in an important text known as the Muratorian Fragment. This is probably a form of introduction to a number of books that its author considered authoritative; the books that he lists are a close match with the canon of the New Testament.[23]

Irenaeus' defence of the fourfold Gospel may be distinguished from the historical processes that gave rise to that fourfold Gospel. Some have argued that Irenaeus played a central and possibly innovative role in establishing the dominance of that fourfold Gospel, others that the way in which he defends it shows that it was already securely established. It is likely that Irenaeus and the author of the Muratorian Fragment lived at approximately the same time, but there is little evidence to inform any judgment as to whether each was independent of each other. If each wrote independently of the other, their apparently similar testimony to the fourfold Gospel may suggest that this development, together with the adoption of the traditional titles of the gospels, took place much earlier in the second century. If not, then one may be an innovator who has influenced the other.

Central to Irenaeus' presentation of the fourfold Gospel is the belief that there is one Gospel in fourfold form.[24] This one Gospel is given in four accounts but is held together by one Spirit. Its giver was the Word, Creator of the world yet manifested to humanity, so it is appropriate that the Gospel is fourfold since the cherubim upon whom he rests are four-faced, their faces being images of the dispensation of the Son of God. Each face is complete in itself, but part of a larger whole apart from which it has no independent existence. Irenaeus' defence of the fourfold Gospel is unashamedly theological. He presents the fourfold Gospel used by the church as a reproach to the heretical groups who reject any one or seek to use only one of its aspects, for in so doing they diminish the one in whom it originates and to whom it bears witness. Irenaeus is aware that individual aspects of this fourfold Gospel originated in particular places and at particular times as the result of the work of individual authors, but claims that all declare only one message: 'that there is one God, Creator of heaven and earth, announced by the law and the prophets; and one Christ, the Son of God' (*Against Heresies*, 3.1.2).

Irenaeus' influence can hardly be overstated. As the first identifiable author whose defence of the fourfold Gospel survives, Irenaeus' conclusions, if not always the details of the arguments on which they rest, have shaped the theory and the teaching of the church ever since. His emphasis on the fourfold nature of the Gospel has neither eradicated the popularity and influence of harmonies such as those of Tatian and of others, or of the tendency of individuals to prefer one gospel to another. Yet, as Rudolf Schnackenburg observes, 'The service that Irenaeus rendered for theology with this establishment of the four gospels is the recognition that in all four gospels Jesus Christ is present as the centre and yet appears in each case in a different form.'[25]

That Jesus is at the centre reminds us that all four gospels are written as witnesses to him. Mark refers either to itself or to its content as the good news of Jesus Christ (Mk 1.1), and Matthew is introduced as the book of the beginning of Jesus Christ (Mt 1.1). Luke begins more allusively, with a reference to the things fulfilled among us (Lk 1.1–4), and although Jesus is neither named nor introduced until after John, it soon becomes apparent that he is the focus of at least the first volume of Luke's account. With John the purpose and focus of his narrative is made clearest of all: 'These things are written that you may believe that Jesus is the Christ the Son of God and that believing you may have life in his name' (Jn 20.31). Here is one Gospel presented in four different forms.

This conviction that there is one Gospel of Jesus Christ, witnessed to by four canonical gospels, raises at least two questions for the way in which we read and preach on the gospels in church. The first concerns the form of the lectionary; the second concerns its content. Both questions are considered in chapter five.

> ## Questions
> Early opponents of Christianity used 'contradictions' between the four gospels in their attacks on the Christian faith, and more recent critics have done so too. How aware are you of differences between the gospel accounts? Do you find the fourfold Gospel a hindrance or a help in learning more about Jesus?

5 Gospel Unity and the Revised Common Lectionary

As we have seen, the Revised Common Lectionary treats each of the synoptic gospels separately, and reads each in conjunction with John.

Therefore the question arises as to whether its *form* (that treats the gospels primarily as individual writings) obscures the conviction that the fourfold Gospel is the pillar that sustains the church. Does it run the risk of setting up four (or three) separate pillars instead? Graham Stanton has contrasted the liturgical adoption of a three-year lectionary cycle with the theological conviction of the fourfold Gospel, asking whether the giving of liturgical priority to the individual writings of the evangelists comes at the expense of the fourfold Gospel: 'Would it not be preferable,' he asks, 'as was the case until modern times, to take seriously in lectionaries Irenaeus' conviction that there is one Gospel in fourfold form?'[26]

Yet it need not follow that a form of lectionary which gives priority to the writings of individual evangelists must detract from the presentation of one Gospel in fourfold form. Those who preach on these texts bear some responsibility for avoiding such drawbacks, but other safeguards such as the structure of the liturgical year also help to demonstrate that the one Gospel which is more important than its vehicles remains constant across the different years of the lectionary. This may be seen in the *content* of the lectionary. A number of examples will serve to illustrate the point. If churches used no synoptic gospels other than Mark in the course of year B, then it is hard to see how Christmas and Epiphany would be celebrated in church. Yet those who have planned the lectionary use Matthew and Luke in all three years, thus accommodating their accounts of both shepherds and wise men, albeit at the risk of the type of chronological harmonizing found both in Tatian and in the Carol Service today. Similarly, all three years include the prologue of John, thus making the point that the Christian doctrine of the incarnation refers to the incarnate life of Jesus, aspects of which are presented in the synoptics as well as in John, even though the former make no explicit reference to that belief. Thus the centrality of the incarnation is anchored in each of the three liturgical years even though there is no explicit account of it in any of the three synoptic gospels which provide the bulk of the gospel readings for each year. Similar points may be made about provision for narratives of the ascension in all three years, when Luke 24 is read in year B (Mark) as well as in Year C.

Other examples might also be given, but the point seems clear that a flexible use of a three-year lectionary based primarily on only one synoptic gospel may be used with discretion and sensitivity to allow that gospel to be seen as one partial witness to a Gospel that is greater than any one individual witness may indicate by himself. Thus Stanton's question is answered by reference to the *content* of the lectionary rather than by its *form*. As actually used, even in a three-year cycle, the lectionary does testify to Irenaeus' conviction that there is one Gospel in fourfold form.

> *Even in a three-year cycle, the lectionary does testify to Irenaeus' conviction that there is one Gospel in fourfold form*

Such considerations of the form and the content of the lectionary and the readings that it includes lead neatly to consideration of the content of preaching on the lectionary. Here the question of whether the treatment of the gospels as individual texts puts too much emphasis on the vehicles of that Gospel rather than on the one to whom they bear witness is raised in a slightly different way. We have seen already that the actual selection of lectionary readings is not dominated entirely by what is or is not included in each of the synoptic gospels, and there is further scope for theological synthesis in the way in which preachers might treat these texts (for more on preaching, see chapter 7).

Questions
- John's gospel is very different from those of Matthew, Mark and Luke. How do you feel about this?
- Does it matter that John is the only evangelist to refer explicitly to the doctrine of the incarnation?

6

The Portrait Analogy

Richard Burridge is an important example of someone who defends the need to let each gospel speak for itself.

Only then, he argues, can we see clearly the carefully crafted portrait of Jesus that each evangelist portrays.[27] Burridge bases his argument on his own important contribution to our understanding of the gospels—his convincing argument that they are best interpreted in their original context as forms of ancient biography.[28] On this basis he offers a helpful discussion of the different ways in which each evangelist has shaped his own distinctive portrayal of Jesus.

Particularly helpful is Burridge's elaboration of the analogy of each gospel as a portrait by reference to four different portraits of Winston Churchill.[29] One shows Churchill, the soberly dressed statesman in conference with Roosevelt; another Churchill the family man at tea with his family; a third presents Churchill in military uniform with British troops; and a fourth as a painter, alone and at peace on the shores of Lac Léman in Switzerland. Each portrait is different, but all recognizably portray one man. Yet, argues Burridge, it is not possible to take elements from all four portraits and fit them together in a fifth. Just as it would be absurd to paint a picture of Churchill entertaining Roosevelt to tea wearing a painter's smock over half a uniform, so attempts to create one master-narrative of Jesus cause us to lose more than we gain. Burridge's point is well-made, and his analysis demonstrates the clear conviction that there is one Jesus behind these four gospels just as there is one Churchill standing behind these four portraits.

Nevertheless, the analogy is not without its difficulties. Were only one of these portraits available, then all we could see would be not only one particular artist's perspective on Churchill but also one particular artist's perspective on one particular aspect of Churchill's character and life at one particular moment. Yet this is quite different from what appears to be the case with any one of the gospels. Certainly it would be foolish to deny that each gospel presents a particular evangelist's perspective on Jesus, just as it would be foolish to claim that any of their accounts set out to be exhaustive.[30]

It is reasonable to argue, however, that each evangelist composed an account that might be considered sufficient to present the ongoing contemporary significance of Jesus on the basis of what he had said and done in the past. There is no reason to suppose that those who painted portraits of Churchill would have thought that their portraits would take the place of and make redundant earlier paintings, yet this is precisely what seems to have been the likely outcome of the writing of a second and third synoptic gospel.[31] Quite possibly John meant his gospel to stand alongside and to supplement at least one of the synoptic gospels,[32] but it is much more difficult to see how any one of the synoptics was ever written to stand alongside the others—even if the church later recognized that all three (plus John) should be placed together.

Most scholars believe that Mark was the first of the synoptic gospels to be written, and that Matthew and Luke each independently used Mark as their primary written source. Matthew pays Mark the back-handed compliment of using almost all of his account, but he adds so much additional material to it that it is difficult to see why anyone would choose to read Mark if they might read Matthew instead. He also makes many changes to what he found in Mark, some of which are of theological significance.[33] Similar points may be made about Luke. He used Mark less comprehensively and apparently more freely than did Matthew, but Luke appears to imply quite openly that there was something unsatisfactory about earlier attempts to provide an orderly account of the significance and events in the life of Jesus and of some of his early followers.[34] The same holds true on other understandings of the literary relationship between Matthew, Mark and Luke ('the synoptic problem').[35] Thus there appears to have been an element of competition in the composition of more than one similar written account of Jesus that was probably not present in the painting of more than one portrait of Churchill. Such competition reminds us of the magnitude of the decision to include four discrete narratives concerning Jesus within one fourfold Gospel. For if each gospel was intended on its own terms to provide a sufficient picture of Jesus, or as full a picture of Jesus as the evangelist wished or was able to portray within the constraints in which he wrote, then the significance of the decision to hold them together can hardly be overstated.

For Oscar Cullmann, the decision to hold these texts together was one of theological necessity. It is precisely because gospels are intended not simply to state historical facts but to proclaim a revealed religious truth based on historical facts that it is necessary to have more than one account. Revelation took place on the human level, but it was impossible for any one person to reproduce it in all its fullness.[36] Thus Cullmann refuses to turn his back on historical explanations for the origin of the fourfold Gospel, a charge that he lays (probably unfairly) against Irenaeus.[37] Cullmann takes full account both of the historical circumstances in which the gospels were written, and also the likely circumstances of their early transmission in different churches whose mutual rapprochement caused them to be brought together.[38] Thus he interprets such historical processes as the outworking of a theological necessity. Cullmann and Burridge are in full agreement that four portraits give a fuller picture of Jesus than any one might do. But neither gives sufficient weight to the likelihood not only that individual gospels were considered sufficient accounts of the significance of Jesus by their authors but also that they were received as such by at least some Christian communities in the period prior to the establishment of the fourfold Gospel.[39]

A second difficulty arises from the comparison of the four gospels with four portraits of Churchill. This is the danger that concentrating too much on different emphases of the evangelists, rather than on their common subject, runs the risk of placing too much emphasis on the evangelists and the way in which they have written their accounts rather than on the one whom they portray. Of course we will be the poorer if we fail to appreciate the way in which each evangelist has selected, arranged and ordered his material so as to tell his story of Jesus in the particular way that best suits the situation in which he writes. We would also be irresponsible if we failed to face up to those points at which they are difficult to hold together in harmony. The plurality of the gospels, particularly within the canon, offers both opportunities and problems for theologians and historians alike, and the church must listen to both.[40] But if we focus on what is distinctive in these texts to the detriment of the one whose story they tell then we will miss the point of what they are doing, bearing witness to the impact and continuing significance of Jesus Christ.

In its worship, as in all aspects of it the life of the church, four gospels are subservient to the one Jesus whom they portray and the one Gospel that shaped—and shapes—the church which preserved the four gospels that it reads. Just as Paul's one Gospel was preached before four (and other) gospels were written and the fourfold Gospel was compiled, so for Christians the one Gospel of Christ crucified and risen remains the key to the interpretation of the four gospels that are its primary witnesses in written narrative form.

> ## Question
> Perhaps a film is more helpful as a modern analogy for the gospels than a portrait. Portraits are static representations that may capture only a particular moment or mood; films allow for development over time and more than one perspective. Many film portrayals of Jesus harmonize incidents and details from different gospels. Pasolini's *The Gospel according to Matthew* is an exception; other exceptions include *The Gospel of Matthew* and *The Gospel of John*, from Visual Bible International.[41]
>
> Which do you think is the best strategy?

Philip Jenson
Preaching the Gospel from the Gospels

7

The discussion about the nature of the gospels and the lectionary has implications for how we tell people about Jesus.

Although the focus in this chapter is on preaching, the same issues are to be found when we retell the story of Jesus in an educational or an evangelistic setting. How can we be faithful to the complex unity of the fourfold Gospel? How can we do justice to the story of the birth, ministry, passion, death, resurrection and ascension of Jesus, the powerful, unified presentation of God's saving love?

a. We should take the lectionary seriously in planning what we say about Jesus. The gospel of the year helps people to be introduced to a particular portrait of him. It might be helpful to begin the year with an overview of the gospel. We should ensure that we (or someone else) do not choose a passage from another gospel at the last moment.

b. The gospel of the year is an invitation to take it seriously at other times, not just on Sundays. Perhaps a series of teaching evenings could be arranged on various sections of the gospel, or the gospel (at least highlights) could be read or performed in one go. For Matthew the superb film by Pasolini could be shown, followed by discussion.[42]

c. One problem with lectionaries and some standard forms of exposition is that they focus on isolated fragments of text. In a world where fewer and fewer know their Bibles well, we may need to relate individual passages much more consciously to the larger story. A brief introduction setting the reading in context might help. But the task of the preacher is (in part) to help hearers encounter the God who has revealed himself through the story of the birth, ministry, passion, death, resurrection and ascension of Jesus. The Gospel is the sum of the parts, and more, an immensely powerful, unified presentation of God's saving love.

d. We should take the lectionary seriously, but not absolutely. The lectionary is a good compromise, but it is still only one way into the Scriptures. The gospel of the year should not determine every sermon. There are, after all, three other readings (do not forget the Psalms!). Further, there is a helpful distinction between 'holy time' (the seasonal festivals), and 'ordinary time,' where there is no clear focus. Ordinary time is an opportunity to plan a sermon series on a particular topic or other book (on this, see Grove booklet W 178 *How to Preach a Sermon Series with Common Worship* by Phillip Tovey). But if a topical series includes reflection on a gospel, then choose this to be the gospel of the year.

e. How do we acknowledge that there is a prior Gospel to which that gospel is but one of several witnesses? One helpful way is to use a varied language when referring to the gospel in a sermon or talk. For example, we are free to use any or all of 'Matthew,' 'Matthew's Jesus,' 'Jesus,' 'the Bible,' or 'the Gospel.' By using different formulations we can do justice to the individuality of each gospel witness, but also to their underlying unity. This implicitly communicates the complex unity of the fourfold Gospel.

f. Explicit as well as implicit reflection on the challenge of the fourfold Gospel will be valuable from time to time. It is increasingly important to explain what is going on in worship, and the challenge of the lectionary can be an introduction not only to the church's reading strategy, but also to more fundamental issues about the nature of the Gospel. This is important, since Christians may well be called upon to defend the accuracy of the gospel portraits of Jesus, which many think to be discredited because of their 'contradictions.'

g. The same tension between the unity and diversity of their witness to God at work is also true of the whole Bible. The gospels constantly orient themselves to the Old Testament, the Bible of Jesus. Each of the biblical books presents a somewhat different and distinctive portrait of God. These come to a unique clarity in the presentation of Jesus in the gospels, but without the Old Testament the language and symbolism of the gospels will not be rightly understood. Even if the focus of the sermon is on the gospel reading, this by no means makes the Old Testament reading superfluous.

h. Nor can Jesus be understood apart from the gift of God's Holy Spirit at Pentecost. The reading from the Epistle bears witness to the continuing work of the Spirit in the church, and helps us to understand a Jesus who is now risen and glorified. A strategy of reading and preaching centred upon the gospels, but informed by both the Old Testament and the Epistles, is essential if we are to testify to the whole counsel of God, Father, Son and Spirit. In this task the lectionary is an enormous help, a gateway into a vast city of variety and coherence, adventure and imagination, with deep wells of refreshment, encouragement and challenge.

Notes

1. For further information, see *The Revised Common Lectionary: The Consultation on Common Texts* (Canterbury Press, 1992). Useful summaries are also available online at http://www.cofe.anglican.org/commonworship/books/interim/lectcommentary.html and at http://commontexts.homestead.com/files/RCL.htm.

2. For an example of a four year lectionary, see the Joint Liturgical Group, *A Four Year Lectionary* (Norwich: Canterbury Press 1992).

3. As Michael Perham observes *(Celebrate the Christian Story* [London: SPCK, 1997] pp 19–20), 'a "year of John" is a difficult diet.' Better, he suggests, is the way in which 'The Fourth Gospel is used in all three years, but especially in the second year, the "year of Mark." Because Mark is a considerably briefer gospel than Matthew or Luke, there is space to read a good deal of John, though it occurs to some extent in the other two years as well. John is used only a little less than Luke, and much more than Mark, over the three years, so the fact that it does not have its own year does not imply any neglect of it.'

4. For a fuller discussion of the differences between the lectionaries of the ASB and of the RCL, and an account of the process that led the Church of England to move from the former to (its own version of) the latter, see Perham, *Celebrate the Christian Story*, pp 17–32.

5. Oscar Cullmann, 'The Plurality of the Gospels as a Theological Problem in Antiquity' in A J B Higgins (ed), *The Early Church* (London: SCM Press, 1956) pp 39–54, on p 40.

6. Graham Stanton, 'The Fourfold Gospel,' *New Testament Studies,* 43 (1997) pp 317–346, on p 318; reprinted in Stanton, *Jesus and Gospel* (Cambridge: CUP, 2004) p 64. Martin Hengel puts the same point more forcefully: 'How is it that we have the narrative of Jesus' activity in a fourfold and often contradictory form in the New Testament and what is the origin of these texts? A single gospel about Jesus would have already spared the church—to the present day—much soul-searching.' 'The Four Gospels and the one Gospel of Jesus Christ' p 14, in C Horton (ed), *The Earliest Gospels: The Origins and Transmission of the Earliest Christian Gospels—The Contribution of the Chester Beatty Gospel Codex P^{45}* (London: T & T Clark International, 2004). This essay is a helpful distillation of Hengel's monograph on the same topic: *The Four Gospels and the One Gospel of Jesus Christ. An Investigation of the Collection and Origin of the Canonical Gospels* (London: SCM Press, 2000).

7   For the origins of this term and its use to refer first to an oral proclamation and then to written narratives about Jesus, see Stanton, *Jesus and Gospel,* chapter two.

8   Graham Stanton, *Jesus and Gospel,* pp 4–5.

9   Graham Stanton, *Jesus and Gospel,* p 5.

10 See Eusebius, *Ecclesiastical History* 6.12.2–6.

11 Irenaeus was Bishop of Lyons in the late second century, and the first clearly dateable and explicit advocate of the fourfold Gospel. His views on the fourfold Gospel are discussed in chapter five.

12 But Serapion does consider 'apostolic' authorship essential, for he excludes from consideration writings that falsely bear the names of apostles. See Eusebius, *Ecclesiastical History*, 6.12.3.

13 The 'rule of faith' is the title sometimes applied to a flexible credal outline of the central beliefs of Christianity in the light of which everything else should be understood. For a general discussion, see D F Wright, 'Creeds, Confessional Forms,' in R P Martin and P H Davids (eds), *Dictionary of the Later New Testament and its Developments* (Leicester: IVP, 1997); on Irenaeus' use of the rule of faith, see F M Young, *The Art of Performance* (London: DLT, 1990).

14 For an introduction to many of these texts, see Hans-Josef Klauck, *Apocryphal Gospels: an Introduction* (London: T & T Clark, 2003). Translations and introductions are available at: www.gospels.net. For a lively and incisive account of their use in recent reconstructions of the historical Jesus, see Philip Jenkins, *Hidden Gospels: How the Search for Jesus Lost Its Way* (New York: OUP 2001).

15 John P Meier, *A Marginal Jew: Rethinking the Historical Jesus. Volume One: The Roots of the Problem and the Person* (New York: Doubleday, 1991) pp 112–166.

16 John Dominic Crossan, *The Historical Jesus: The Life of a Mediterranean Jewish Peasant* (Edinburgh: T & T Clark, 1991) pp 427–450.

17 Luke Timothy Johnson, *The Real Jesus: The Misguided Quest for the Historical Jesus and the Truth of the Traditional Gospels* (San Francisco: Harper Collins, 1996) pp 44–50, quotation on p 47. Johnson's critique is highly polemical, but its substance may be found in other more balanced critiques of Crossan. See, for example, Mark Allan Powell, *The Jesus Debate: Modern Historians investigate the life of Christ* (Oxford: Lion, 1999) pp 93–110; Hans-Josef Klauck, *Apocryphal Gospels*, pp 2–3. On the *Gospel of Peter* Klauck concludes: 'Recent attempts (see Crossan) to identify and distil from [the *Gospel of Peter*] the oldest stratum of the passion narrative, on which the New Testament gospels too would have based their accounts, do not stand up to a closer examination of the texts.' (*Apocryphal Gospels*, p 87).

18 *Against Heresies* 3.11.7, *cf* 3.11.9

19 Oscar Cullmann, 'Plurality' p 48, citing Origen, *Commentary On John* 5.7.

20 See further, Richard Burridge, *Four Gospels, One Jesus?* (London: SPCK, 1994) p 165.

21 On the relationship between John and the Synoptics, see D Moody Smith, *John Among the Gospels* (Columbia: University of South Carolina Press, 2001).

22 See especially Richard Burridge, *What are the Gospels? A comparison with Graeco-Roman biography* (Cambridge: CUP, 1992; Second Edition, Grand Rapids: Eerdmans, 2004); *idem, Four Gospels*, pp 166–171.

23 On all these developments, see Stanton, 'The Fourfold Gospel.'

24 For what follows, *cf* Irenaeus, *Against Heresies* 3.11.8. See also T C Skeat, 'Irenaeus and the Four-Gospel Canon,' *Novum Testamentum* 34 (1992) pp 194–199, reprinted in J K Elliott (ed), *The Collected Biblical Writings of T C Skeat* (Leiden: Brill, 2004).

25 Rudolf Schnackenburg, *Jesus in the Gospels* (Louisville: Westminster John Knox Press, 1995) p 14.

26 Stanton, 'The Fourfold Gospel' p 345. In the revised version of this article, reprinted in *Jesus and Gospel*, Stanton appears to have modified his position. There (on p 90) he writes: 'Most churches in the United Kingdom have adopted a three-year cycle in which a whole year is devoted to each of the synoptic gospels, with passages from John's gospel inserted at appropriate points. Is this compromise satisfactory? I think that it probably is, though extended use of the new pattern may prove otherwise.' For arguments why the three-year cycle is better than a four-year alternative, see above, n 2.

27 Burridge, *Four Gospels,* pp 164–166.

28 Above, note 22.

29 Burridge, *Four Gospels* pp 1–2, 163.

30 Note the explicit disclaimer of the fourth gospel (Jn 20.30–31) which, in its canonical context at the end of the fourfold Gospel, might be taken to refer not just to John but also to the fourfold Gospel in its entirety. See David Trobisch *The First Edition of the New Testament* (New York: OUP 2000) pp 96–101.

31 Leslie Houlden, *The Strange Story of the Gospels: Finding Doctrine through Narrative* (London: SPCK, 2002) pp 17, 20, 111.

32 See for example Richard Bauckham, 'John for Readers of Mark,' in *idem* (ed), *The Gospels for All Christians: Rethinking the Gospel Audiences* (Edinburgh: T & T Clark, 1998) pp 147–171.

33 Houlden, *Strange Story*, pp 44–56, 109.

34 Houlden, *Strange Story*, pp 63–67.

35 On the Farrer-Goulder hypothesis, Matthew uses Mark, and Luke sets out to use and to supplant them both. If Markan priority is rejected and Mark is thought to have conflated Matthew and Luke in order to mediate between them and to reconcile or to remove their differences, then it is unlikely that he will have wanted his account to have been read alongside theirs.

36 Cullmann, 'Plurality' p 50.

37 Cullmann, 'Plurality' pp 51–52.

38 Cullmann, 'Plurality' p 46.

39 Cullmann accepts that the gospels were probably used initially in this way, prior to the mutual rapprochement of various churches ('Plurality,' p 46), but implies that such use was inadequate. Burridge does not address this point, but may perhaps imply it, albeit in passing, when he notes (*Four Gospels*, p 175) that some have argued that the four gospels were each written for different audiences.

40 See Robert Morgan, 'The Hermeneutical Significance of Four Gospels,' *Interpretation* 33 (1979) pp 376–388.

41 For details of these films, and further resources on the Bible in film, go to: www.ntgateway.com/film/

42 And, of course, there is John Proctor's helpful Grove Biblical booklet B 32 *Matthew's Jesus* to accompany such an exercise!